DATE DUE

GAYLORD			PRINTED IN U.S.A.

THE HYDROSPHERE

THE AGENT OF CHANGE
HYDROSPHERE

GREGORY L. VOGT, Ed.D.

TWENTY-FIRST CENTURY BOOKS · MINNEAPOLIS

Text copyright © 2007 by Gregory L. Vogt

Twenty-First Century Books
A division of Lerner Publishing Group
241 First Avenue North
Minneapolis, Minnesota 55401 U.S.A.

Website address: www.lernerbooks.com

Library of Congress Cataloging-in-Publication Data

Vogt, Gregory.
    The hydrosphere: agent of change / by Gregory L. Vogt.
       p.   cm. — (Earth's spheres)
    Includes bibliographical references and index.
    ISBN-13: 978-0–7613–2839–1 (lib. bdg. : alk. paper)
    ISBN-10: 0–7613–2839–4 (lib. bdg. : alk paper)
    1. Water—Juvenile literature. 2. Hydrology—Juvenile literature. I. Title.
  II. Series: Vogt, Gregory. Earth's Spheres.
    GB662.3.V64 2007
    551.46—dc22   2006014879

Manufactured in the United States of America
1 2 3 4 5 6 – DP – 12 11 10 09 08 07

CONTENTS

PLANET OCEAN

Imagine yourself as an alien from outer space visiting Earth for the first time. You pilot your starship into the solar system and head in the general direction of the Sun. You whiz past giant planets, slip by some asteroids, and zero in on a smallish blue planet with white clouds. It is the third planet outward from the Sun, and it is called Earth. As you approach it, you see rocky continents beneath the clouds and huge polar ice caps. However, the thing that most catches your attention are the great expanses of liquid water. Fully 70 percent of Earth's surface is covered with vast rolling oceans.

Liquid water on the surface of a planet is a great rarity in the solar system and throughout the galaxy as well. One of the reasons for this is based on the fact that water can exist in three states—solid (ice), liquid, and gas (steam). Which state water exists in is determined primarily by temperature. For pure liquid water, the temperature must be no less than 32°F (0°C) and no higher than 212°F (100°C). Below 32°F, water will freeze, and above 212°F, water will boil. Throughout the galaxy, planets near stars are usually heated well above the boiling point and farther planets are chilled well below freezing. There is only a narrow distance range around every star where temperatures are just right for liquid water. Earth orbits around its star, the Sun, in the middle of that perfect temperature zone.

 Water is shown in its three states— gas, liquid, and solid. The states are determined by how closely the molecules are packed together.

THREE STATES OF WATER

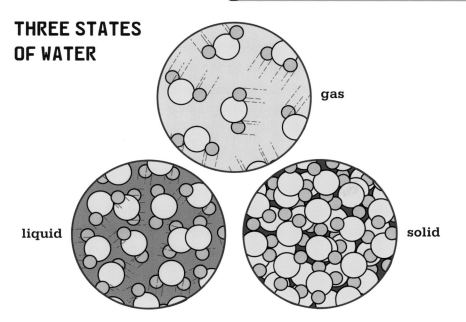

gas

liquid

solid

Temperature isn't the only thing that has to be just right for liquid water to exist. There has to be a strong gravitational field in order to hold an atmosphere of gas. The weight of Earth's air exerts pressure on its surface. Without pressure, water quickly boils even at low temperatures. If Earth were too small to hold an atmosphere, any oceans it may have once had on its surface would have boiled away long ago. Earth would be like the Moon instead.

Earth's oceans are just one part of a number of complex and interrelated systems that make up the planet. Like an egg with a yoke, white, and a shell, Earth is made up of spheres, one on top of another. The inner sphere, called the core, is made up of iron and nickel metal. The outer layers of the core are molten, but its center is solid. Movements of the molten part of the core generate magnetic fields that reach through the upper layers of Earth out into space. The core is surrounded by another sphere called the mantle, which consists of molten, solid, and semisolid rock. Heat from the mantle and core is carried to Earth's surface by molten lava that cools as it spews out and piles up to create new land. Resting on the semisolid upper edge of the mantle is the lithosphere, which consists of a thin crust of solid rock that makes up the continents and the ocean floor. The rising heat currents and rock from the mantle exerts pressure on the lithosphere, causing it to spread apart in some places and sink in others. The currents in the upper mantle cause the continents to move slowly about Earth's surface.

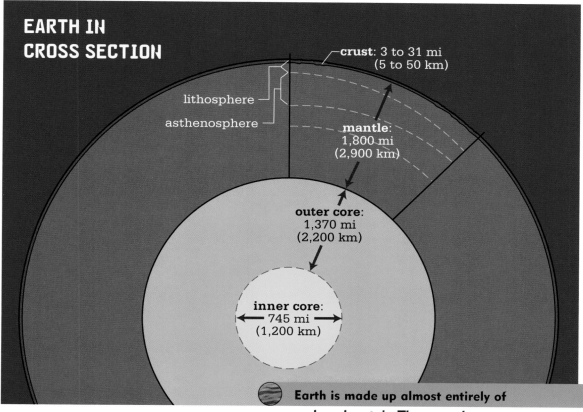

EARTH IN CROSS SECTION

crust: 3 to 31 mi
(5 to 50 km)

lithosphere

asthenosphere

mantle:
1,800 mi
(2,900 km)

outer core:
1,370 mi
(2,200 km)

inner core:
745 mi
(1,200 km)

 Earth is made up almost entirely of rock and metal. The water layer or hydrosphere covering most of Earth's surface is far too thin to appear in this cross-section diagram showing Earth's layers.

Above the lithosphere are three spheres that intermingle with one another. These spheres are more like zones where important things take place. There is the hydrosphere, consisting of all of Earth's surface water, ice, water vapor suspended in the air, and water soaked into the ground. The zone of living things found on the surface is called the biosphere. Then comes the atmosphere, which is a thin layer of air completely surrounding Earth. The atmosphere is a complex mixture of different gases and swirling clouds made of water drops or ice crystals. The final layer of Earth is the outer atmosphere. This is the uppermost and thinnest part of the atmosphere where space shuttles and space stations travel as they orbit the planet. It is where the entire Earth system first interacts with the great energy source of the solar system, the Sun.

This book, one of six on Earth's spheres, tells the story of Earth's hydrosphere. It is a complex tale with many parts. The part of Earth that is the hydrosphere is a relatively tiny part of Earth as a whole. Almost all of Earth is rock and metal. Nevertheless, the hydrosphere has a profound impact on the surface of the planet and the processes that go on there.

Hydrosphere water makes up a relatively thin outer layer surrounding Earth. In the deepest part of the oceans, a place near the Pacific Ocean islands of Guam and Yap called the Mariana Trench, the water layer is about 7 miles (more than 11 kilometers) thick. Overall, Earth's oceans average about 2.3 miles (3.8 km) in depth. On the land, water collects in rivers and lakes and soaks into the soil. In the high elevations and the polar regions, water is found as snow and ice. Snow and ice covers the tops of many of Earth's mountains including Earth's tallest mountain, Mount Everest. This massive mountain, part of the Himalaya range in Nepal, stretches upward to about 5.8 miles (9 km) above sea level. At an even higher elevation, water in the form of tiny droplets and ice crystals swirls through the air as clouds. Water is also found within rock itself on the ocean floors and in the rock of continents. Rock

The peak of Mount Everest is the highest spot on Earth. Here, water occurs as snow and ice and also as droplets and ice crystals forming clouds.

such as sandstone, for example, is made of grains of sand cemented together. It can be very porous. Water readily soaks into this kind of rock. If rock is cracked and fractured, water will seep down into the cracks. As a result, water can be found several thousands of feet beneath the surface of the rocky crust in many places around the world.

From the lowest to the highest point, Earth's hydrosphere is roughly 20 miles (32 km) thick. That is equal to about one-half of 1 percent of Earth's total diameter. Put another way, if Earth were a basketball, the hydrosphere would only be as thick as the tiny rubber bumps on its surface. Though not very thick when compared to the whole planet, the hydrosphere nevertheless has a tremendous influence in the other spheres of Earth.

CHAPTER 1

WATER, WATER, EVERYWHERE

Everywhere you look
on Earth, you find water.
It covers the entire planet in
one form or another. Water is
found in oceans and rivers, in wisps of
clouds, and in snow and ice fields. It saturates the soils
of Earth and fills up the cells of all living things.
Although widespread, the majority of Earth's water supply resides in just one place. Earth's oceans are a vast
water storehouse containing about 97 percent of the
planet's total water supply.

Ocean water evaporates and later falls to the surface
of the continents as rain and snow. Because the continents rise above the oceans, rain and snow meltwater, propelled by gravity, gradually slides off the
land surface and returns to its ocean source.

A great, planetwide water cycle is at work, stirring both oceans and atmosphere. We will make a detailed examination of this cycle later.

Hydrosphere water can be divided into two main kinds—seawater and freshwater. The difference between these two waters is their chemical composition. Seawater has many chemicals that were washed off the land and dissolved to give the water a strong salty taste. Freshwater, the water we drink, has few dissolved chemicals, and the water is usually tasteless. We will see in a moment why water acts as a dissolving agent.

Water itself is a simple molecule consisting of two atoms of hydrogen and one atom of oxygen. Atoms have electrical charges that cause them to attract and bond to

About 97 percent of Earth's water is in the oceans and is too salty to be used for drinking or industry. Approximately 3 percent is freshwater, the majority of which is frozen in ice caps and glaciers.

one another. The two hydrogen atoms in a water molecule sit next to each other on one side of the larger oxygen atom. When diagrams of a water molecule are drawn, they look like the head of Mickey Mouse. The oxygen atom is the face, and the two hydrogen atoms make up the ears. Scientists classify a water molecule as dipolar. The hydrogen atoms on one side of the molecule have positive charges, and the oxygen atom to the other side has a negative charge. The negative side of one water molecule attracts the positive sides of another water molecule. You have seen this effect many times. When rain falls, vast numbers of water molecules cluster and stick together to form raindrops. Raindrops that run down a windowpane creep together to form bigger drops as they stream downward. The attraction of water molecules for one another tries to pull drops into the shape of spheres. Gravity

When two atoms of hydrogen bond with one atom of oxygen, they form a water molecule. Because the hydrogen atoms lie next to each other on one side of the oxygen atom, the molecule has a positive charge on one side and a negative charge on the other.

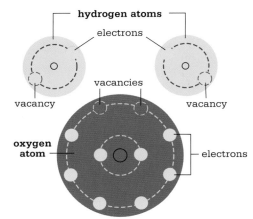

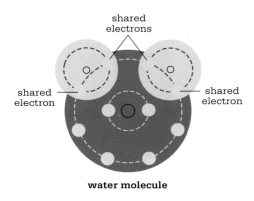

THE WATER MOLECULE

water molecule

A raindrop's size determines its shape. Drops with a diameter of .04 inch (1 millimeter) tend to be round, while larger drops become flatter and thus elongate as they fall.

interferes with this and flattens them out somewhat. You can get a good look at the water drop shape and gravity's effect on this shape by placing water drops on a piece of wax paper. In Earth's orbit, where gravity's effects are reduced, water makes beautiful spheres of all sizes. They fascinate astronauts. Nearly every astronaut movie from space shows them playing with globes of water.

The dipolar nature of water molecules makes water great for dissolving things. The charged sides of water molecules will attract and tug on the molecules of other chemicals such as sodium chloride, which is known to you as table salt. The attraction of the water molecules literally pull apart salt molecules so that they become ions of sodium and chlorine mixed in with the water molecules. Ions are electrically charged atoms.

ICE FLOATS!

Water is one of the few substances that becomes less dense when it freezes. Most materials become denser as they approach their freezing temperature. Water does too until it reaches the temperature of 39.4°F (4°C). At that point, until it is frozen solid, the water molecules begin packing themselves in very orderly arrangements called a crystalline structure. The molecules actually spread a little more apart as they freeze than when they are in liquid form. As a result, ice is less dense than water and it floats. Ice is about 9 percent lighter than an equal volume of water. When you see an iceberg floating in the open ocean, it may not look very big. Beneath the surface is a chunk of ice about nine times bigger than the ice above the surface.

As water cools, it contracts, and the molecules move closer together. Near the freezing point, the molecules move apart again. When they freeze into a rigid pattern of crystals, the ice is less dense than liquid water. Thus, ice floats.

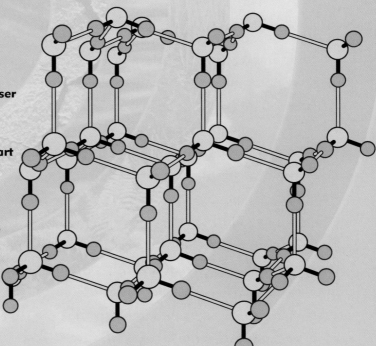

ICE CRYSTALS IN A LATTICE FORMATION

As a result, when you pour grains of salt into a glass of freshwater, the grains disappear. If you let the water evaporate, the sodium and chlorine ions recombine and all that is left is a coating of salt on the inside of the glass.

Much of Earth's water is seawater. It is a chemical mixture of a wide range of materials. After the water itself, the largest component of seawater is salt. Every pound of seawater contains about 0.5 ounces (30 grams per kilogram) of sodium chloride. You can simulate seawater by adding 0.25 ounces (7.1 g, or 1 rounded teaspoon) of table salt to an 8-ounce (237-milliliter) glass of water. The taste is not pleasant, but it is not harmful if this amount is all you drink. Sailors adrift in lifeboats are strongly cautioned about drinking seawater. The salt content of the water will actually cause their bodies to dehydrate, and they will be much thirstier than they would be if they had drunk no seawater at all.

In addition to the sodium chloride, seawater has another 0.08 ounces (5 g/kg) of other chemicals dissolved in every pound. The other main chemicals are magnesium, sulfate, calcium, potassium, and compounds such as bicarbonate. There are also trace amounts of other chemicals, including iron and gold, in seawater. Depending upon where you are, seawater may also contain pollutants from human activities.

The concentrations of dissolved chemicals in seawater can change from place to place. In the polar regions, seawater freezes to form ice caps, but the presence of

Composition of Seawater

Chemical Ion Contributing to Seawater Salinity	Concentration in Parts per Thousand in Average Seawater	Proportion of Total Salinity
Chlorine	19.345	55.03
Sodium	10.752	30.59
Sulfate	2.701	7.68
Magnesium	1.295	3.68
Calcium	0.416	1.18
Potassium	0.390	1.11
Bicarbonate	0.145	0.41
Bromide	0.066	0.19
Borate	0.027	0.08
Strontium	0.013	0.04
Other	less than 0.001	less than 0.001

dissolved chemicals has an effect on the freezing temperature. Pure water freezes at 32°F (0°C). Seawater actually freezes at about 28.4°F (−2°C). As it freezes, seawater rejects the dissolved chemicals, making the ice very pure. (Chunks of sea ice are great in iced tea!) The freezing process works from the surface downward as the polar seas cool off in winter. The rejected chemicals increase the concentration of chemicals in the seawater beneath the ice. This condition reverses itself in the spring, when ice melts on the upper surface of the pack. The freshwater runoff mixes with the saltier seawater and returns its dissolved chemical composition back to normal.

Chemical concentration in seawater is also adjusted by freshwater from rivers emptying into bays and coastal wetland areas. The addition of freshwater dilutes the salt content of the water there.

Chemical concentration is further changed by evaporation. See this for yourself by taking your glass of artificial seawater and letting the water evaporate on a sunny windowsill over a few weeks. The water will be gone, but the salt will coat the inside of the glass. Boiling salty water does the same thing, only faster.

Solar energy warms the oceans, and water evaporates into the atmosphere. It leaves behind the dissolved chemicals. The pure water vapor later becomes rain and snow. The world's entire freshwater supply begins as salty ocean water.

HEAT ENGINE

Water stores heat. Scientists call this ability heat capacity. Water has one of the highest heat capacities of any substance. Oceans and the world's largest lakes store so much heat energy from the Sun that they moderate the entire planet's climate as it goes through its yearly seasons. Without this stored heat, the atmosphere would become extremely cold in the hemisphere experiencing winter and very hot in the hemisphere experiencing summer. The average global ocean temperature is 38.4°F (3.6°C), but local temperatures vary widely.

Though surface ocean temperatures might be near freezing along the far northern North American continent edges in winter, the water still contains a great amount of stored solar heat. Some of this heat is transferred to the air above, making it warmer than it would be otherwise. When weather systems move this air over the land, the air moderates winter temperatures. In summer the water temperature is much lower than the summer air temperature over the heating land. The oceans have a cooling effect. People living along coastal regions look forward to the cool ocean breezes that come with summer.

LAYERS

Looked at from the side, ocean water forms two distinct layers—surface water and deepwater. The surface layer is thin, only about 330 feet (100 meters) deep, but it is a very active place.

Surface water has many interactions that keep it stirred. Winds drive the water by creating waves that cross oceans and currents that run along shorelines. The Sun creates vertical warm and cold currents that circulate throughout the surface layer in a manner like the circulation in a simmering pot of soup. Earthquakes, fractures in the lithosphere, create powerful waves that spread rapidly across oceans and smash shorelines. Differences in global temperatures generate currents that lace the oceans at all levels. Earth's daily spin bends ocean currents in clockwise directions in the Northern Hemisphere and counterclockwise directions in the Southern Hemisphere. The combined gravitational attractions of the Moon, Earth, and the Sun create tides that raise and lower water levels on Earth as these two bodies orbit each other. The surface-water layer is a busy place.

The surface-water zone is where the bulk of living things that inhabit Earth reside. Huge forests of kelp and microscopic floating plants capture the Sun's energy so that they can grow. Plants in the surface-water zone

Giant kelp, which can measure up to 200 feet (61 m) high, can form underwater forests, which provide food and shelter for fish.

provide food for microscopic animals, which in turn feed larger animals in a great chain of food, of which we are a part. In the growing process, plants release oxygen that filters into the atmosphere to refresh it while absorbing carbon dioxide from the air.

The temperature range in the surface-water zone varies greatly with latitude. In the equatorial or tropical latitudes, water temperature can range in the 70s to 80s°F (21 to 26.6°C). Along some continental edges, such as the western sides of North and South America, cold-water currents from higher north and south latitudes chill coastlines. Far north and far south, the temperature drops close to or even below freezing.

DEEPWATER LAYER

The deepwater layer is very different from the surface-water layer. It is a very stable, quiet zone within the ocean. Wave action and tides have little effect in the deep-water. The chemical composition in this layer is pretty much the same all over the world. The water is much colder than surface water, and temperatures are very constant regardless of latitude. As you plunge to the depths, sunlight fades and all becomes black. The plant life that is common in the surface layer can't survive in the deep-water layer beneath the light zone. Dead plant matter and animals will sink to the bottom and slowly decay and dissolve, releasing rich nutrients into the water.

About 0.5 mile (0.8 km) beneath the surface, the water temperature ranges from about 42 to 46°F (6 to 8°C). Below 1.2 miles (2 km), the water is nearly constant at 39.2°F (4°C) all the way to the bottom.

Although the deepwater layer is much more stable than the surface layer, there are currents present. These currents originate in the polar regions. The Arctic deep current generally flows south from the polar regions to the equatorial region. The Antarctic bottom current generally flows northward. More will be said about currents later.

FRESHWATER

The world's freshwater supply, only about 3 percent of Earth's total water, is really recycled ocean water. Coming down as rain and snow, it spreads out and collects on the land surfaces of Earth. Depressions in the surface fill up with water to become ponds and lakes. Some of the water turns into ice and becomes glaciers and polar caps. Some of the water soaks into the soil as groundwater. It may remain there for hundreds of thousands of years. Eventually, groundwater breaks out in springs or is sucked up in wells for drinking, agricultural, and industrial uses.

FROZEN RESERVOIRS

Mountain glaciers are rivers of ice. Like rivers of liquid water, glaciers flow down valleys, and as they do, they grind, scour, and chip away rock. Because these glaciers are solid ice, everything takes place in slow motion. However, over time mountain glaciers cut deep U-shaped valleys. Eventually, the ice creeps down into lower valleys where the climate is warmer, or they may flow all the way into an ocean. If the toe of a glacier reaches the ocean, large chunks of the toe of the ice calve, or break off. Winds and water currents may float the chunks out into the oceans where they become icebergs. It is at the toe of the glacier that the ice begins its conversion back into liquid water.

Not all glaciers reach the sea. Many of the world's rivers start out as mountain glaciers. Because the ice primarily melts in the summer when it is warmer, the flow in these rivers continues even through the driest periods of

RISE AND FALL OF POLAR ICE

At any one time, sea ice covers as much as 15 percent of Earth's surface. When it is winter in the Northern Hemisphere, the Arctic ice cap grows and thickens. At the same time, Antarctica experiences summer. The edges of the Antarctic continental glaciers break off and float away as giant icebergs. The situation reverses when it is summer in the north. The Antarctic ice regrows while the Artic ice thins and some breaks up into small icebergs.

the years. Many towns and farming areas depend upon glaciers for their water supply just as other places employ water towers.

Mountain glaciers are found in high mountainous regions where the climate is generally very cold. Some of the best locations for mountain glaciers are far north and far south of the equator. Alaska and British Columbia have many, as do Russia and northern Europe. Mountain glaciers are found in the far southern reaches of South America as well. All told, the mountain glaciers of the world add up to about 386,000 cubic miles (1.6 million cubic km) of ice.

To start forming a mountain glacier, more snow has to fall in a depression or valley on the slopes of a mountain than melts off in the summer. Over many years, the thickness of the snow mounts up. Near the bottom of the pile, the snow is compressed and air pockets are driven out. Eventually, the snow crystals fuse together to become ice. As more snow accumulates, the thickness of the ice layer at the bottom increases. Eventually, the weight of the ice becomes so great that it starts to spread out like very slow-moving pancake batter. It would spread out in all directions, but the shape of the valley controls its movements. Because of gravity, the ice starts to flow down the valley, carrying with it any loose sediment and rock in its way. The ice becomes very dirty. As it continues to flow, the debris it carries grinds the valley floor and walls, making the valley wider. In places where the rock is softer, shallow basins are scooped out. Much later, if the world's climate gets warmer and glaciers melt, these basins become strings of small lakes on the valley floor.

When snow accumulates over broad regions, huge masses of glacial ice can form. During long periods of colder-than-normal climates, large continent-sized glaciers form and spread out to completely cover the northern ends of North America and Eurasia. Such a period began about one million years ago and is called the Great Ice Age. Ice repeatedly spread southward from the north and then retreated during warmer periods. As recently as ten thousand to twenty thousand years ago, glacial ice more than 1 mile (1.6 km) thick slowly ground its way over the

GREENLAND IS MELTING

Greenland, the world's largest island, is a frozen world with 85 percent of its surface covered with ice and snow. After Antarctica, Greenland hosts the world's second-largest mass of frozen water. Preliminary measurements indicate the Greenland ice cap is melting and thinning due to climbing world temperatures. The temperature rise is affecting many of the world's glaciers. They are retreating back up their mountain valleys as more ice melts off their toes in summer than accumulates in the upper regions in winter. Glaciers are like a thermometer for the world. Their melting indicates a global warming trend that could lead to all sorts of changes including sea level rise, loss of animal and plant species, and droughts in some areas and flooding in others.

northern United States. Only Antarctica is still covered with continental glaciers, and except for mountain glaciers, the north ends of North America and Eurasia are glacier free. But we may only be in the middle of an interglacial period. Another climate shift could start the glaciers coming again.

CHAPTER 2

ROUND AND ROUND AND ROUND

The next time you drink a bottle of water, try to imagine where that water came from. The label on the bottle will say that it came from some very pure spring or from some deep well. There will be pictures of mountains and forests on the label. It all looks very pure and clean. The fine print may say that the water has been put through some miracle filtering process to assure the finest quality. But where did the water really come from? When you drink water, it is not gone. Some of it becomes part of your body for a time, and some leaves as waste. Water, like all matter, cannot be destroyed. It can be broken down into atoms of hydrogen and oxygen, which will eventually combine into water again. The molecules of water in that water bottle are ancient!

Those molecules may have fallen to Earth in a collision with a comet billions of years ago. They may have steamed out from Earth's mantle along with lava during ancient volcanic eruptions. Over eons of time, those molecules became a part of glaciers, rained down on the land during great hurricanes, passed through the bodies of dinosaurs, roared along the Colorado River, and carved out the Grand Canyon. They returned to the oceans countless times, passed through the gills of fish, and soaked into the soil to eventually be collected as the bottled water you are drinking. The story doesn't end there because the water leaves you as body waste and continues its journey. In a few years, you might end up buying some of the same water molecules again!

The movement of water around Earth is one of Earth's biggest systems. The movement is called the hydrologic cycle. Like any circle, there really isn't a beginning and an end. Nevertheless, we need to pick a starting point, and ocean water will do. The driving force of the cycle is solar energy. The Sun delivers tremendous amounts of heat and light energy to Earth. When the Sun is high in the sky, the energy warms the ocean surface water and speeds up evaporation. Evaporation is the process by which liquid water turns into a gas. Countless trillions of molecules evaporate from the surface and enter the atmosphere every second. The molecules are wafted higher and higher into the atmosphere until they encounter colder air. Earth's atmosphere is dusty. Tiny dust particles are stirred by wind and lofted around the planet. The microscopic

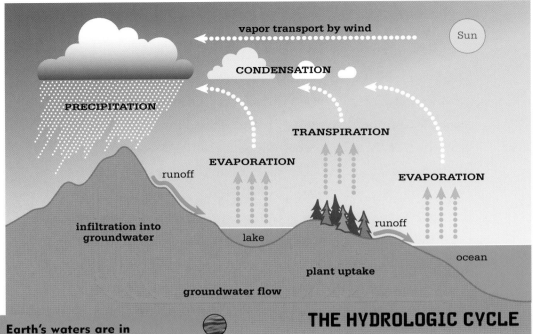

vapor transport by wind

Sun

CONDENSATION

PRECIPITATION

TRANSPIRATION

EVAPORATION

EVAPORATION

runoff

infiltration into
groundwater

lake

runoff

ocean

plant uptake

groundwater flow

THE HYDROLOGIC CYCLE

Earth's waters are in continuous motion as evaporation moves water from the oceans into the air. Water falls back to the land as precipitation, and then back to the oceans again.

particles come from volcanic erup-tions, forest fires, dust storms, and human-made pollution. As the evap-orated water molecules chill down, they try to return to the liquid state. To do so, they need something to attach themselves to. Water begins condensing on atmospheric dust particles, forming tiny droplets of liquid water.

Meanwhile, winds, stirred by the Sun's energy, push the growing droplets around the world. Eventually, so many droplets are floating in the air that they become visible as white clouds. The shapes of the clouds mark the movements of the air currents. In time, the droplets grow so large that air currents can no longer support them. The droplets fall as rain and recombine with ocean water. If the droplets make it over land before falling, the drops splash on the hard surface and either soak into the soil to become groundwater, get sucked up in plant roots, evaporate, or run off and collect in rivers and lakes. Depending upon the

UP AND DOWN

Because of gravity, the surface of the ocean in any part of the world is about the same distance from Earth's center. This is referred to as sea level. Sea level is really an average altitude of the sea surface because there are some differences around the world. The surface at the equator is bulged a few miles higher than polar ocean water because of Earth's spin. Finally, the level is also affected by tides and winds. In spite of the bulges, the average elevation of the oceans is used as a reference plane for mapping Earth's surface shape. How high is a mountain? The elevation is measured from sea level no matter where the mountain is on Earth. How deep is a valley? Again, the elevation is measured from sea level. In a few places around Earth, valleys are actually lower than sea level. Mountains or other landforms that keep the oceans from flooding in surround these deep valleys. The elevations of these deep valleys are given in negative numbers.

The lowest point of the Western Hemisphere lies in southeastern California's Death Valley—282 feet (86 m) below sea level.

season, how far north and south of the equator the droplets are, and their elevation above the surface, they may freeze before falling and become snow or ice crystals.

Water that falls on the land surfaces of Earth gradually works its way back to the oceans. This includes water that soaks into the soil. Gravity pulls the water downward into cracks and pores until the water reaches the water table. The water table is similar to what you would get if you filled a glass of water with sand and then poured in some water. The water will settle in the bottom of the glass and fill all the pores between the sand grains. At some level above the bottom, the sand will be dry. The interface between the dry and the wet sand is the water table.

The water in the water table is called groundwater. Groundwater is used extensively for drinking and agricultural purposes. Wells are drilled and pumps inserted to raise the water to the surface. However, there are many places where the shape of the land or the amount of groundwater present causes the water to seep out on the surface. These water seeps are called springs. Spring water will either evaporate or join runoff water in rivers. Either way, the water eventually returns to the ocean to complete the cycle.

The hydrologic cycle has many loops in it. The water may turn into ice and become part of a glacier or an ice cap. The water can remain in this state for many tens of thousands of years before it continues on its journey.

POWER FOR SPACEFLIGHT

Using electricity, water molecules can be separated into atoms of oxygen and of hydrogen. If brought back together with a little heat, the two recombine. The process is called oxidation. Another word for it is burning. Hydrogen and oxygen burn very quickly, and this makes them a great fuel for spacecraft. The space shuttle has three main engines that are powered by hydrogen and oxygen. The two gases are sprayed into combustion chambers in the engines where they burn explosively. Flames and billowing white clouds shoot out of the engines. The clouds are not pollution but consist of water droplets, just like natural clouds in the atmosphere.

Although the exhaust emission from a departing rocket looks quite dramatic, the huge white clouds are just what they appear to be— clouds, a formation of water droplets, just as we see in the sky overhead.

Rainwater, falling on the land, is also absorbed by plant roots. The plants use the water to build plant cells for growth. Water is an important ingredient in the process of photosynthesis. Green plant cells take in sunlight, water, and carbon dioxide from the atmosphere. The plants create sugar for plant growth, release oxygen into the atmosphere, and give back some of the water to the atmosphere in a process called transpiration. Water retained in the plant cells is eventually transferred to animals that eat the plants. Waste processes and decay ultimately return the water to the cycle.

CHAPTER 3

GROUNDED!

We don't think much about ground-water because we can't see it in the ground. Water that seeps into Earth fills in the pore spaces between grains of soil and the spaces between grains of rock such as sandstone. It also seeps into bubble holes in volcanic rock and into cracks in dense igneous rocks, such as granite. The only time we actually see groundwater is when it leaves the soil and rock and comes to the surface to temporarily rest in lakes and swamps or to flow in rivers. Groundwater may seem to be static and dull, but it is anything but that.

Groundwater is found virtually under all land surfaces on Earth. In dry desert regions, the water table, or upper surface of the groundwater, may settle 1 mile (1.6 km) or more beneath the surface. In wetter areas of Earth, the water table will be found just 10 to 20 inches (25 to 50 centimeters) beneath the surface. Where the water table reaches the surface, springs, rivers, lakes, and swamps are found.

Although it may appear that water that seeps into the ground after a rain is gone for good, it is not. Instead, it joins a very complex system beneath the surface that is in slow but constant motion. In time, perhaps tens of thousands of years, the water will

Groundwater is water that has soaked into the soil and moved into the pores of underground rock. An area where there is a significant amount of groundwater is known as an aquifer. The level of underground water is called the water table.

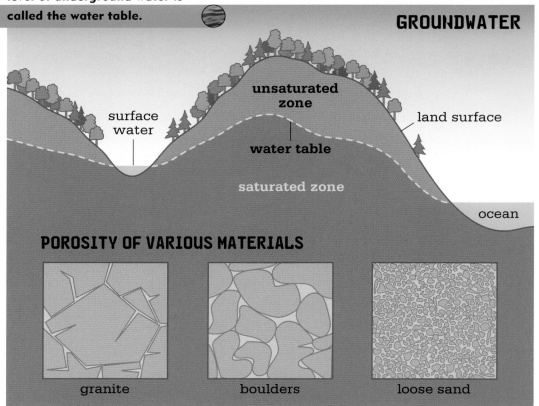

GROUNDWATER

surface water

unsaturated zone

land surface

water table

saturated zone

ocean

POROSITY OF VARIOUS MATERIALS

granite

boulders

loose sand

make its way back to the surface to return to the oceans and begin a new journey.

When rain or snow falls (and later melts), some of the water flows off immediately or evaporates. The rest sinks into the ground. How much sinks in depends upon the kind of surface the water fell on. If the water falls on a sand dune, much of it will soak right into the sand. If it falls on a granite mountain, most will run off. The key is the porosity of the material that the water falls on. Loose sand has many pore spaces to hold water, while granite may only have minute cracks to hold the water. Porosity is one of two important factors that determine how water sinks into the surface.

The other factor is permeability. Permeability sounds a bit like porosity, but there is a difference. Permeability refers to how easy it is for water to move through soil and rock. Of course, this depends upon the size of the pores. Rocks can be very porous but water still may have a hard time moving through because the pores are tiny. Rocks such as shale can have lots of pores, but you need a micro-scope to see them. A rocklike conglomerate, which is made up of pebbles cemented together, can have large pores that water easily pours through. To see the relationship be-tween porosity and permeability, try this experiment. Get two identical paper cups, a pin, a sharp pencil, and some water. Punch about twenty pinholes into the bottom of one cup and a single hole with the pencil tip into the bottom of the other. Punch the holes from the inside of the cups. The area of all the pinholes together will be about the same as the area of the pencil tip hole. Both cups have the same porosity. Fill both cups with water to about 0.5 inch (1 centimeter) deep, and see which one empties first. The cup with the larger hole has the greater permeability.

Once water soaks into the ground, it does amazing things. First, it continues moving, although the rate of movement may be very slow. The place where the water enters the ground is called the recharge zone. Any place can be a recharge zone as long as enough rain or snow falls and the surface has pores so that some water soaks in.

TAKE A BREAK

Water flowing on the land surface occasionally takes a break. It collects in basins to become lakes. Lakes are bodies of water that are completely surrounded by land. Most lakes are small and cover just 12 or more acres (4.9 hectares) of land. They dot the landscape in many parts of the world. A few lakes are huge, such as the five interconnected Great Lakes in the United States and Canada or such as Lake Baikal in Russia. Lake Superior of the Great Lakes is the largest freshwater lake in the world. It has a shoreline that runs 2,800 miles (4,508 km). Lake Baikal, however, is the deepest lake. In one place, Lake Baikal's bottom is more than 1 mile deep—5,370 feet (1,637 m).

Lake water comes from rain and snow and from rivers that flow into them. The water remains for a while and mixes with other lake water before it flows away through outlet rivers or just evaporates back into the atmosphere.

Gravity pulls the water downward, but as the water reaches the water table, the water no longer goes downward. Instead, it starts to spread out. Unlike a dining room table, the water table is rarely perfectly flat. Instead, the water-table surface mimics the shape of the land it is under. The water table beneath a hill is shaped like a hill, though not as high. Beneath a valley, the water table takes a valley shape. Gravity pulls on the water and slowly moves it down subsurface inclines in the water table toward the nearest ocean, where it ultimately ends up at sea level.

DEEP PLACES OF THE WORLD

Because water is a dipolar molecule, it is able to dissolve some of the minerals in the rocks it passes through. Water readily picks up carbon dioxide from the atmosphere. Although it still looks like water, the presence of carbon dioxide turns water into a mild acid (carbonic acid). Two kinds of rocks are especially susceptible to water when it becomes acidic—limestone and dolostone. Groundwater in these two rocks will eat away at minerals, enlarging the pores. More water gets in, and more minerals are dissolved, and so on. In places where limestone and dolostone are cracked, the acidic water easily passes downward along the cracks. The dissolving goes on at a greater rate, and the cracks widen. Since these two rocks are sedimentary, they will have horizontal surfaces, called

WORLD'S LARGEST UNDERGROUND LAKE

The world's largest underground lake is a water-filled lead mine in Bonne Terre, Missouri. The old mine passages and rooms carved out of limestone rock stretch 1 mile (1.6 km) north to south and 2 miles (3.2 km) east to west. Pillars of limestone keep the ceiling of the mine from collapsing into the lake. People actually use the lake for water sports.

bedding planes. This is where the rock is slightly different due to temporary climatic changes during rock formation. Dissolving may progress along the planes as well. Gradually, a system of interconnecting tunnels form caves. Caves can grow huge networks of passages at many different levels. Mammoth Cave in Kentucky, for example, has more than 30 miles (50 km) of known passages.

If drier times occur, most of the water in cave systems will drain out. Slow-moving underground rivers may flow along the cave floor and exit on the surface along canyon walls. If the groundwater dissolves away large chambers of rock near the surface, the surface may collapse creating a sinkhole.

In time, a fairyland of strange rock formations forms inside caves. Water drops rich in dissolved minerals cling to the ceiling of caves and slowly evaporate. The water drops leave behind some of the minerals that crystallize back into rock. More water drops seeping down from the rock above cling in the same spot and leave their dissolved minerals. Gradually, over tens or hundreds of thousands of years, huge icicle-like rock formations grow downward toward cave floors. These are called stalactites. Meanwhile, other water drops fall to the floor and gradually build up blunt piles of rock that are called stalagmites. In time, the stalactites and stalagmites grow together to form columns in caves.

HOT SPRINGS AND GEYSERS

Some of the most spectacular sights around the world are hot springs and

Mammoth Cave in Kentucky, part of the world's longest cave system, was formed as acidic water trickled through cracks in limestone, eventually wearing it away. Stalactites and stalagmites are a dramatic side effect of this erosion.

geysers. These occur where there has been recent (in geo-logic terms—thousands of years ago) volcanic activity and the rock is still very hot. Groundwater seeps down into cracks and pore spaces and becomes heated to well above boiling temperatures. That's because increased pressure at this depth increases the boiling point of water just as decreased pressure lowers it.

If the crack system is fairly open, the hot water rises and seeps out onto the surface. The water has acquired chemicals that dissolved into it when it was deep beneath the surface. As the water spills out, it cools and these chemicals crystallize to form rock. The rock builds up successive rims around the seep, and it becomes a pool of hot, steaming water called a hot spring.

If the crack system is deep and narrow, an explosive condition may build up. Relatively cool surface water seeps into the piping and comes into contact with very hot water at this depth. The weight of the cooler surface water on the deep water acts like a cork. The deepwater becomes superheated from the surrounding hot rock. At first, steam bubbles try to form, but the pressure causes them to col-lapse. Gradually, the surface water is heated from below. When all the temperatures are just right, steam bubbles form again and begin escaping to the surface. They push out some of the surface water, and this lowers the pressure on the superheated deep water. Steam bubbles explosively form and rush to the surface, driving the remaining water above with great force. The hot water blasts out of the ground like a fire hose. It is something like popping the top off a warm soft-drink bottle that has been shaken too much. Instead of a hot spring, this crack system forms a geyser. After the eruption, the ejected water begins seeping back into the crack to repeat the eruptive process.

Geysers are rare around the world. There are only about one thousand of them worldwide, and about half of

YELLOWSTONE NATIONAL PARK

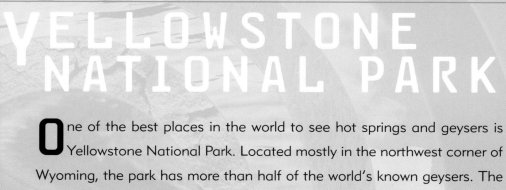

One of the best places in the world to see hot springs and geysers is Yellowstone National Park. Located mostly in the northwest corner of Wyoming, the park has more than half of the world's known geysers. The biggest is Steamboat Geyser, which can shoot water up to 400 feet (122 m) into the air. When Steamboat Geyser erupts, it is a great sight, but few people have the pleasure of seeing it because the interval between eruptions can be anywhere between four days and fifty years. Sometimes the eruptions are at night. Old Faithful is much easier to see because it erupts every 35 to 120 minutes.

A geyser *(right)* can be compared to a volcano. While volcanoes spew out melted rock from deep below Earth's surface, geysers erupt water.

them, such as Old Faithful and Steamboat Geyser, are in Yellowstone National Park.

ROLLING ON THE RIVER

Not all rain and snow meltwater soaks into the ground. Some of it is pulled off the land surface and collects in rivers. At high elevations, rivers tend to be small but very fast moving. As the land slope becomes more gradual, water velocities decrease. The movement of water in rivers affects the shape of the land. Like glaciers, rivers erode the land by carrying away soil and pushing rocks and sand grains that grind and wear away river bottoms. Because liquid water flows much more rapidly than ice, erosion caused by rivers is comparatively rapid. Valleys in mountainous areas are steep walled and V shaped. Where river water runs slower, valleys widen.

Rivers start out small, but because their channels twist and wind, small rivers collide and join to become larger rivers. Consequently, rain and water from melting snow and ice over a large region, called a watershed, eventually combine into a single river that empties into the ocean. All the sediment carried by the river is dropped in large triangular-shaped deposits called deltas.

While standing upon the bank of a river, such as the Mississippi River, it is easy to get the idea that rivers are a big part of the hydrosphere. They are an important part of the hydrologic cycle, but at any one time, the amount

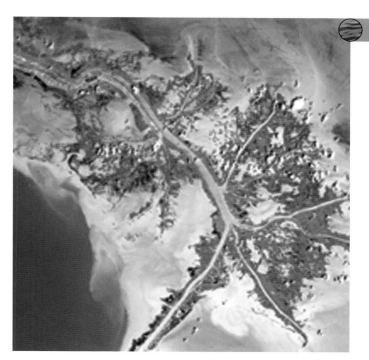

Deltas, such as the Mississippi River Delta shown here from the air, are formed when rivers flow into larger bodies of water and their ability to carry sediments is suddenly reduced.

of water carried by rivers is really very small. Compared to the entire supply of water in the hydrosphere, rivers only make up 0.0001 of 1 percent of the total. However, as insignificant as the total quantity of river water seems, rivers provide the majority of the freshwater used by the people on Earth for drinking, washing, agriculture, and industry.

CHAPTER 4

OCEANS
IN MOTION

The world's oceans are constantly moving. Water moves in all compass directions and up and down. It doesn't take much to get water moving. Friction from wind blowing across its surface causes ripples that grow into huge waves. Earthquake vibrations propel powerful waves that span oceans and smash against distant shores. Differences in water temperatures and densities create currents that flow across the surface, creep along ocean bottoms, and sink and rise. The driving forces behind ocean water motion include the Sun, Earth's rotation, the Moon's gravity, and, on rare occasions, large earthquakes. These motions stir the surface layer of the ocean and gradually propel deep water around the globe.

WAVES

Waves are the most obvious example of oceans in motion. The primary cause of waves is wind. Friction with the air, as it blows across the water surface, creates small ripples that travel in parallel lines perpendicular to the wind direction. Wind ripples are easy to make. Just blow across the top of a soup bowl filled to the brim with water. Ocean ripples start out very small, but once they form, they grow in size. The water surface is no longer smooth, and the high spots in the ripples catch more wind. With added energy from the wind, the tops, or crests, of small waves get higher while the valleys, or troughs, sag deeper. The stronger the wind, the bigger the waves become.

The actual motion of waves is somewhat surprising. Except for when waves slide up and crash on shorelines, the water in waves doesn't move very much. You can see this if you watch floating debris. A cork or a fishing bobber in the open ocean moves up and down as a wave passes. Its horizontal motion, driven by wind or water currents, is much slower, and it can take many months to drift even short distances.

Oceanologists, scientists who study ocean dynamics, create large tanks to study wave motion. The tanks are like very long and narrow swimming pools with glass or plastic sides. A wave generator on one end creates waves that roll down the tank to the shallower water at the other end. Small floating markers in the water show how the water moves as waves pass by. Oceanologists observe that as a wave passes, the markers move up and down in a circular pattern. The energy of the wave passes through the water while the water itself remains pretty much in the same place.

If you have ever been snorkeling, you will know that while on the surface, you bob around like a cork as the wave passes. However, if you dive to the bottom, you hardly feel passing waves at all. The depth that wave energy reaches is determined by the wavelength of the waves. Wavelength is the distance from one wave crest to another. The rolling motion of the wave only reaches down about half the distance of a wavelength. For example, if the wavelength of two successive waves is 100 feet (about 32 m), then the wave energy is only felt down to a depth of about 50 feet (about 16 m).

Across open oceans, waves don't have much effect on anything unless a major storm like a hurricane is at work. Powerful hurricane winds can magnify open

Friction with the wind causes waves to travel across ocean surfaces. The waves take on a curve shape that rises above and below the calm sea surface. Wavelengths are measured from wave crest to wave crest, and wave heights from the lowest to the highest point.

OCEAN WAVES

crest

wavelength

crest

wave height

calm sea

ocean waves to frightening pro-
portions. A movie called *The
Perfect Storm* (2000) was based
on an actual incident that took
place on Halloween in 1991.
Three storm systems combined
their forces over the North Atlantic
Ocean. At times, wind speeds topped
120 miles (193 km) per hour, and waves as
high as a ten-story building were reported.

The volume of the water in the world's oceans is approximately 317 million cubic miles (1 billion 321 million cubic km).

When waves approach shorelines, water motion
change dramatically. Oceanologists observe this action in
their wave tanks. As the wave begins moving up the
slanted surface of the tank that simulates a shoreline, the
circular motion of the wave changes. The lower part of the
circle starts dragging on the bottom while the top of the
circle keeps on going. The circle becomes egg shaped.
Finally, the wave top flops over and crashes on the incline.
The wave creates a swash of turbulent water that rolls up
the shoreline until its energy is dissipated. Then the water
flows back down the shore slope in a backwash. The same
thing happens on all the beaches of the world.

Small waves simply wash up on the shore and slide
back, but big waves are something different. The energy
accumulated by big waves as they cross the seas pounds
the shoreline. The force is great enough to smash rocks and
grind the pieces into sand grains. With each wave, the
grains roll up and back as the water recedes before the next

wave arrives. Waves are a major force shaping the world's coastlines. In some locations, like the north shore of the Hawaiian island of Oahu, really large waves can build up that attract surfers from around the world. The waves can roll so much that they curl over on themselves and make a tunnel of water that the best surfers love to slide into.

If all shorelines were straight, incoming waves would be very uniform in size. However, walk along an ocean shoreline that is curved or has rocky points, and all kinds of interesting things can happen. A bay, or inward curved coastline will cause the line of waves to curve and spread out their energy. Points of land cause waves to wrap around them and concentrate their energy with pounding force. Rocky sea cliffs have places that act like funnels to capture lots of wave energy and concentrate them in small areas. Wave splash will rocket high up these chutes.

TSUNAMIS

Not all waves are wind driven. Some are caused by subsurface disturbances such as earthquakes, submarine landslides, or even large meteorite impacts. These waves are called tsunamis, a Japanese term, or seismic sea waves. When a disturbance takes place, these waves are generated and they can travel across thousands of miles of ocean. These waves pack tremendous energy and travel as fast as a jetliner, 300 to 500 miles (500 to 800 km) per hour, but they are almost invisible in the open ocean. The wave height (elevation difference between the trough and the crest) might be as much as 6.5 feet (2 m), but the wavelength will be about 600 miles (1,000 km). The wave crests are so far apart that the wave slope itself is almost flat. A tourist on a cruise ship wouldn't even feel a bump as the wave crest passed. However, when the waves reach shallow water, the tremendous energy they contain produces huge waves that first pull back the shallow water in harbors, leaving a muddy flat. Moments later, waves towering 50 feet (15.2 m) or more slam into the shoreline, shatter coastal villages, and sometimes drown thousands of people.

Monster waves 100 feet (30 meters) high sometimes form in the ocean and are thought to be the cause of more than 200 supertanker sinkings since the 1980s.

OCEAN CURRENTS

Just about everybody has heard about the Gulf Stream current circulating clockwise in the North Atlantic Ocean. Ocean travelers would steer their ships into the current if traveling from the United States to Great Britain and avoid the current when returning. Riding the Gulf Stream is like riding a raft down a river. The speed of the Gulf Stream water shortened Atlantic passages by many days.

THE GREAT TSUNAMI

I t was just before eight on the morning of December 26, 2004. People living around the rim of the Indian Ocean were fishing, washing clothes, working the fields, having breakfast, or shopping. Their lives were about to change. About 18 miles (29 km) beneath the ocean, along the margin of two massive crustal plates near Indonesia, a slippage occurred. Normally, these plates creep against each other a distance of about 2 inches (5 cm) a year. This morning, one of the plates practically leaped over the other a distance of 50 feet (16 m). It was a massive earthquake that sent tremors throughout Earth. This was only the start of the tragedy.

With the crustal shift came a huge mass of ocean water that was propelled outward in concentric rings. Traveling hundreds of miles per hour, the waves were barely noticeable in the open ocean, but when they approached shorelines, it was another matter. Racing up the shallowing ocean bottoms to the shore, the waves reached towering heights, scraping clean shorelines of buildings, trees, and people. More waves followed. By the

Tsunamis can cause massive loss of life and property destruction in coastal regions in their paths. The most devastating tsunami in modern times began in the Indian Ocean on December 26, 2004. It caused a circular pattern of devastation, as the wave hit the shores of Indonesia, Malaysia, Thailand, India, Myanmar, and Sri Lanka.

time the water had receded, as many as 230,000 people had been crushed or drowned by the waves in a dozen countries. Millions were left homeless, and wreckage was scattered everywhere.

These waves are called tsunamis from the Japanese word meaning "great harbor wave." Tsunamis have occurred on many ocean shores throughout the history of Earth. Tsunamis more than 1,000 feet (305 m) high have crashed on ancient shores. On April Fool's Day, 1946, a tsunami was generated by an earthquake in the Aleutian Trench off the coast of the Alaskan island of Unimak. Hours later, residents of Hilo, Hawaii, were startled to see the ocean completely retreat from the harbor, stranding fish in the mud. Some ran out to pick up the fish, little knowing that an approaching tsunami was gathering its strength. They should have sought higher ground. A 60-foot-high (18 m) wave slammed into the harbor, smashing dozens of residents to their deaths.

53

There are many other, less famous currents winding their way across the oceans of the world. Some currents ride near the ocean surface while others creep along ocean floors. When surface currents collide with continents, they are either deflected to one side and curve away or dive downward. Deepwater currents may also curve or be driven upward toward the surface by landmasses.

Currents are propelled by tides, differences in seawater density, and by wind. Tides are caused by the gravitational pulls of Earth, the Moon, and the Sun working with the orbital motion of Earth and the Moon around the Sun. Tidal currents are most noticeable in shallow-water areas, especially where the land creates natural funnel shapes that force large amounts of water through narrow passages. Slow-moving tidal currents can grow

The world's oceans continuously move in patterns known as currents. Currents result from wind acting on surface water as well as from the differences in temperature and in salt content of water on the surface and in deeper waters.

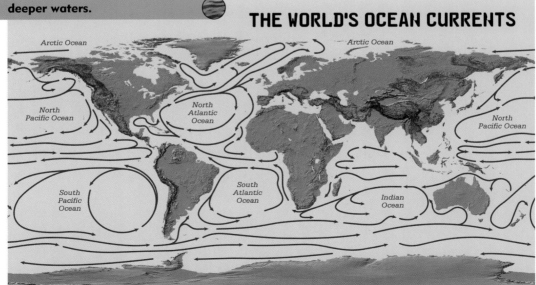

THE WORLD'S OCEAN CURRENTS

Arctic Ocean

Arctic Ocean

North Pacific Ocean

North Atlantic Ocean

North Pacific Ocean

South Pacific Ocean

South Atlantic Ocean

Indian Ocean

to raging torrents if they get squeezed into small areas. The effect is something like the way a garden hose squirts water. Open the nozzle wide and the water bubbles out. Narrow the nozzle opening and a powerful stream of water shoots across the yard.

Differences in seawater density create very large ocean currents. Seawater with a high content of dissolved chemicals (salinity) is denser than seawater with low salinity. Therefore, water with high salinity sinks beneath water of low salinity. We learned earlier that when seawater freezes in the Arctic and Antarctic, the ice ejects dissolved chemicals. This increases the salinity of the water beneath the ice. That makes the water there denser, and it slowly sinks to the bottom. The denser water begins piling up on the bottom, and it spreads southward in the Arctic and northward in the Antarctic. This creates deepwater currents that move toward the middle latitudes. When the currents approach shorelines, the currents may rise to the surface in what is called a coastal upwelling. Coastal upwellings are very beneficial because the currents bring tremendous amounts of ocean bottom nutrients to the surface. The nutrients support large sea life communities and are important fishing areas for the world's food supplies.

Water temperature is another factor in ocean currents. Warm water is less dense and rises up over more dense cold water. Water warmed in the midlatitudes spreads out on the surface of the oceans. The Gulf Stream is a warm surface current that starts near the Gulf of Mexico and

DENSITY CURRENTS

Cold water is denser than warm water. You can see this quite easily for yourself. Mix food coloring into a small amount of cold water. Very gently add the cold water to the surface of a clear glass of hot water from the faucet. The cold water will stream to the bottom of the glass. The same thing happens when cold milk is added to hot coffee. You can reverse this by filling a glass with cold water and marking some hot water with food coloring. Suck about half a drinking straw full of the hot water, and hold it in the straw with suction from your mouth. Push the straw to the bottom of the cold-water glass, and gently blow the hot water out of the straw. The hot water will rise to the top. As a result of density differences, there is little mixing between surface water and deep water. Try the experiment again, but replace the hot water with salty water. Add food coloring to the salty water, take a sample of it with the straw, and release it into the clear water.

heads northeastward between Iceland and Great Britain. As it moves northward, the warm Gulf Stream interacts with the colder water. Gradually, the Gulf Stream cools and sinks and turns southward as a cold deepwater current.

WIND CURRENTS

Earth's atmosphere is a major player in the creation of ocean currents. We have already examined how wind produces waves. The drag of wind across water can also create surface ocean currents that actually move large masses of water across oceans. Prevailing winds (winds constantly moving in one direction), driven by unequal heating of Earth's surface, tend to blow westward between the latitudes of 30 degrees north to 30 degrees south. Winds above and below 30 degrees tend to go to the east. If Earth did not have any landmasses, ocean currents would follow the winds and circle the world. The deflection of currents by landmasses, as well as other factors, affects the direction of major wind-driven currents. Those in the Northern Hemisphere tend to travel in a large clockwise direction loop, and currents in the Southern Hemisphere loop in a counterclockwise direction.

The surface current system is pretty complicated because of all the things that get involved. One of these things is called the Coriolis force. The force is created by Earth's rotation.

Earth rotates from west to east about an axis extending through its interior from the North Pole to the South Pole. Because Earth is a sphere, the equator sticks out farther from this axis than does the Arctic Circle. A point on the equator travels in a bigger circle than does a point in Great Britain, for example. Since both points make complete circles in twenty-four hours, the equator point travels faster than the point in Great Britain because it has a greater distance to cover. The difference in rotation speeds at different latitudes cause warping of both ocean currents and atmosphere storms. (Have you noticed how hurricane clouds spiral in satellite pictures?)

Let's focus on a single ocean current in the North Atlantic Ocean that we have already discussed—the Gulf Stream. We will follow it as it heads from the Gulf of Mexico region northward. Because the Gulf water is fairly near the equator, it is moving rapidly eastward due to Earth's rotation. As it heads northward, it encounters slower-moving water. The momentum of the Gulf Stream water causes it to curve eastward through the slower northern ocean water. Eventually, the Gulf Stream is deflected by the Europe landmass and some of it bends back to the south. Its speed has dropped because it is mixing with the slower North Atlantic Ocean water. As the Gulf Stream aims back

In the Northern Hemisphere, winds blow around the eye of a hurricane in a counterclockwise direction (as shown in this satellite photo of Hurricane Katrina). In the Southern Hemisphere, they blow clockwise.

THE GULF STREAM

Gulf
Stream

NORTH
AMERICA

EUROPE

Gulf of
Mexico

North
Atlantic
Ocean

AFRICA

EQUATOR

The Gulf Stream is a swiftly moving clockwise system of currents that effects climate, sea transportation, and the circulation of ocean nutrients in the North Atlantic Ocean.

to the south, its lesser momentum causes the current to curve westward back toward the Gulf of Mexico.

The Coriolis force is one of the main reasons why the Gulf Stream and other currents in the world's oceans travel in loops. Ocean currents are very complicated, and the loops can be confusing to look at. When currents collide, drag against one another, warm up or cool down, bump into continents or islands, or . . . Well, you get the idea.

When ocean currents are mapped on a globe, they look like a continuous worldwide freeway system with main corridors, ramps, and overpasses and underpasses. A warm current crosses an ocean, cools and sinks, and becomes a cold current, which turns and rises elsewhere and becomes a warm current again and so on. However, unlike a freeway system in a city, ocean freeways can change.

EL NIÑO

Midlatitude winds, called the trade winds, normally blow westward over the Pacific Ocean. The trade winds drive warm surface-water currents toward Australia and Indonesia. The water piles up, and sea level there is actually about 1.5 feet (0.5 m) higher at Indonesia than Ecuador and Peru in South America. The surface water at Indonesia is about 14.4°F (10°C) warmer than it is along the western coast of South America. The surface flow westward encourages cold deepwater currents to rise (coastal upwelling) along the coast of Ecuador and Peru.

Every few years, in the event called El Niño, the trade winds relax so that the currents drop off and the piling up of water toward Indonesia diminishes. Without the surface water being pulled away from the western South America coastline, the coastal upwelling that brings deepwater nutrients to the western edge of South America slows. Gradually, a massive pool of warm seawater spreads eastward across the Pacific and arrives at South America.

Though temporary, El Niño causes all sorts of problems. Without a strong coastal upwelling of cold water along South America, the surface water warms, and this leads to greater evaporation and increased rainfall in such places as Peru and even the southern United States. The reduction in nutrients from the coastal upwelling reduces ocean plant growth, and this impacts the ocean food chain. Fishing boats end up with smaller catches. In really strong El Niño years, flooding and extensive mudslides can devastate rural and urban areas. The other side of the Pacific has its problems too. Rainfall amounts drop, and droughts in Australia and Indonesia occur. When the westerly trade winds pick up again, things go back to normal.

SHORE CURRENTS

When waves strike ocean shorelines, they usually do so at some angle other than straight on. The wave front hits the shoreline along one end of the beach and works its way along the beach to the other. This angular wave front propels water at the beach edge in a direction parallel to the shore. A longshore current is created. The strength of the current depends on how big the waves are. As the current flows, it carries sand grains. This isn't usually a problem because other sand brought in from somewhere else replaces sand that is carried away. The beaches sometimes get narrower or even washed away during big storms, but new sand is deposited there later. However, in many tourist locations, sandy beaches are an important attraction. City and resort developers will place long piles of rock and concrete that stretch out into the water to block longshore currents. Rather than saving their beaches, the rock piles, called jetties, often focus the energy of waves and create stronger currents that scoop out more sand on one side of the jetties and dump it on the other side. This makes for a very irregular shoreline.

A jetty is a breakwater, usually made of timber and stone or just stone. It is used to break the force of rough waves.

TIDES

We speak of sea level as though it were constant. The elevations of the world are measured from the ocean water surface, but as stated before, the surface used for this measurement is actually an average. Furthermore, the actual elevation of the sea at any particular point is not constant. It continually changes. Tie a rowboat to a pier in shallow water off an ocean shoreline and come back in a few hours. The boat may be resting on the beach even though it didn't move. Fall asleep sunbathing near the water's edge and you may wake up surrounded in water. A pretty complicated series of factors that include the gravity, Earth rotation, orbits, and the shape of ocean shorelines cause these temporary sea-level changes, called tides.

The Moon stays in orbit around Earth because of the gravity of Earth and the Moon pull on each other.

OCEAN BASIN SHAPE

Ocean basins start with a continental shelf. This is the gradual slope of the continental plate edges as they descend into the water. At a depth of about 426 feet (130 m), the underwater edge of the continents drop more sharply in what is called the continental slope. Many thousands of feet down, the bottom levels off. This is called the abyssal plain. Except for occasional deep trenches, abyssal plains are the deepest part of the oceans. On the other side of the ridge, the water drops back to the abyssal plain and then climbs upward to the shore of the continent on the opposite side of the basin. The diagram below is most typical of the North and South Atlantic Ocean basins. The bottom rises sharply in a submarine mountain range called the Mid-Atlantic Ridge. Although following the same general characteristics, the Pacific Ocean basin exhibits a far more complex pattern of undersea mountain ranges than the Atlantic.

In the Atlantic Ocean basin, a global submarine mountain range known as the Mid-Atlantic Ridge snakes along the ocean floors for about 50,000 miles (80,000 km).

AN OCEAN BASIN

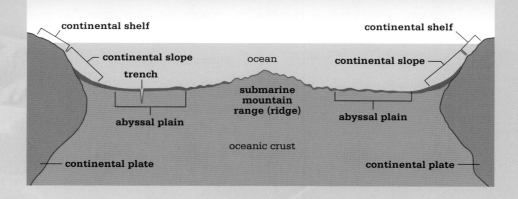

continental shelf

continental slope

trench

ocean

continental shelf

continental slope

submarine mountain range (ridge)

abyssal plain

abyssal plain

continental plate

oceanic crust

continental plate

If that was all that was going on, most of the water in the world's oceans would be drawn to the side of Earth nearest the Moon and the far side of Earth would be dry. There would be just one tide. Instead, there are two tides, one on the near side and one on the far side of Earth. What is going on? The answer has to do with the Moon's orbit.

The Moon takes about twenty-eight and a half days to orbit Earth. Diagrams of this usually show the Moon traveling in a circle with Earth at the center of the circle. That is not entirely accurate. Every day, the Moon's orbit changes its position in the sky about 12 degrees to the East—but there is more. Imagine that gravity were a solid bar connecting Earth and the Moon. Then imagine that you could toss them in the air like a baton. You would see Earth and the Moon revolve around each other. The Moon, being smaller and lighter, would swing in a big circle, while the far heavier Earth would swing in a small circle. The point about which the two bodies revolve is actually a spot within Earth about 1,100 miles (1,770 km) from the surface.

What does the Moon/Earth rotation have to do with tides? Take a bucket and put some water in it. Start the bucket swinging, and eventually swing it in a big circle that crosses over your head. The water stays in the bucket even when it is upside down because of centrifugal acceleration. Something similar is happening on Earth. The Moon's gravity pulls ocean water so that it bulges the ocean in the direction of the Moon.

BAY OF FUNDY

Shoreline shape plays an important part in determining the height of ocean tides. Long, gentle shorelines usually have tides that rise and fall only a few feet. When shorelines are shaped like funnels, tides can pile up higher in the middle. One such place is the Bay of Fundy, in Nova Scotia near the Canada-Maine border. At low tide, the bay is drained of water and fishing boats wallow in the muddy tide flats. As high tide approaches, water is funneled into the bay. A wave, called a tidal bore, rushes into the bay, and in a short time, the water level rises 33 feet (10 m). When conditions are just right, the water level can rise as much as 52 feet (16 m)! Fishing boats lift off the muddy flats as the water level rises. The Bay of Fundy has the world's highest tides. In other areas, such as the Seymour Narrows in British Columbia, the tidal bore can reach velocities of 14.4 miles (20 km) per hour in extreme conditions. That is about three to four times faster than you can run.

Tides rise and fall according to the gravitational pull of the Moon. Water gradually rises for about six hours until it reaches the high-tide point and then falls for about the next six hours until it reaches the low-tide point. At the Bay of Fundy, the rise and fall is particularly dramatic as seen in these two photos of the same waterfront scene, six hours apart.

Because of centrifugal acceleration, a second tide bulge is created on the far side of Earth. These bulges are called high tides. Places halfway between the two high tides, where the water was drawn from, are lower and are called low tides.

In addition to the rotation of Earth and the Moon system, Earth also rotates. This causes the locations of the high and low tides to change. When the Moon rises in the East, because of Earth rotating eastward, the high tide follows. (The high tide is not directly beneath the Moon because Earth's continents and friction with ocean bottoms slow it down a bit.) The high tide on Earth's opposite side also follows the Moon's position. So when you stand on an ocean shoreline and the Moon rises, high tide rolls in and raises the water level. You have to back up to keep from getting wet. By the time the Moon has set in the west, the tidewater has begun receding and you can walk back to where you were before. However, you don't have to wait for the Moon to rise for the next high tide. When the Moon is on Earth's far side, another high tide rolls in. Every day there are two high and two low tides.

At different times of the year, the actual levels of high and low tides can change. In addition to the gravity of Earth and the Moon, the Sun's gravity also affects water levels. Tides are highest when Earth, the Moon, and the Sun are in direct line with one another. These are called spring tides. When the Moon is 90 degrees away from the Sun, high tides are lower and are called neap tides.

CHAPTER 5

BURNING RIVER

A strange thing happened in Cleveland, Ohio, in 1969. A stretch of the Cuyahoga River just southeast of downtown caught fire. The fire raged for about twenty minutes until three fire battalions on the banks and a fireboat crew were able to extinguish it. In the course of the blaze, flames, estimated to be as much as five stories tall, damaged two railroad trestle bridges that spanned the river. One bridge was so charred that the heat warped even the steel rails. Of course, it wasn't the river water itself that was burning. It was an industrial discharge of highly flammable petroleum-based chemicals onto the water surface that burst into flames. This was the river's third fire. One of the earlier fires caused extensive riverbank damage.

When a 1969 fire on the Cuyahoga River captured national attention, *Time* magazine described it as the river that "oozes rather than flows" and in which a person "does not drown but decays." The fire spurred a massive environmental cleanup.

The Cuyahoga was one of the most polluted rivers in the United States. It was described in a magazine article at the time as "chocolate-brown, oily, bubbling with subsurface gases, it oozes rather than flows." Cleveland had already begun a cleanup of the river when the third fire struck. The attention the fire received nationally helped in the passage of important federal laws to protect and improve rivers. Although the Cuyahoga River has been restored, many of the world's rivers, lakes, and even the oceans are endangered by human activity.

Long ago, the capacity of rivers to absorb and carry away waste from industry, mines, and homes seemed limitless. Sewer pipes, resting on riverbanks, emptied directly into the water. The water flow carried away human sewage, chemicals, oil, trash, fertilizers, and silt. The philosophy was simply "out of sight, out of mind." Although never good for rivers and the creatures inhabiting them, the rivers did their job. The pollution ultimately ended up in the oceans where it dispersed with little effect. That, of course, was a time when the people of the world only numbered in the millions. More than six billion people compete for Earth's freshwater supply. Although recognized as absolutely essential for life, many water systems around the world have been fouled by human activity. Furthermore, in many places, notably the arid countries in Africa, freshwater is in short supply.

More than a billion people around the world do not have adequate access to clean water. Contaminated water spreads diseases, such as dysentery and cholera, that are especially hard on young children. Some of the polluted water is the result of chemicals and toxic elements from industrial processes. Fertilizer and pesticide that run off from farms around the world are absorbed by the fatty tissues of fish and passed up the food chain to humans. Oil spills in the oceans kill fish, marine mammals, and birds. Heavy pumping of groundwater in urban and agricultural areas has seriously lowered water-table levels, forcing such cities as Los

By far the largest users of freshwater resources are thermoelectric power plants and irrigation systems.

The *Exxon Valdez* oil spill on March 23, 1989, had a profound effect on the Alaskan waters, killing thousands of animals immediately. Despite the massive cleanup, even more wildlife died from aftereffects in the years that followed.

Angeles to have to import water through aqueducts from across the state and from nearby states.

But the problem is not just having enough clean water for drinking. Water is an important part of the world's food supply. A ton of wheat takes about 1,000 tons of water to produce. About 40 percent of the world's food supply comes from irrigated water. That's water pumped from the ground or from rivers. The demand for irrigation water in Idaho is so great that the Snake River dries to a trickle and the scenic Shoshone Falls actually shuts off in summer. Other rivers of the world have also run dry because of a combination of irrigation uses and drought. The water in the Yellow River in China failed to flow as far as the ocean for 226 days in 1997.

WHERE IS THE WATER?

Location	Volume	Percent of Earth's Total Water	Remarks
Oceans	317,000,000 mi³ 1,321,256,000 km³	97.217	Salt water
Ice	7,000,000 mi³ 29,176,000 km³	2.146	Mostly in the Antarctic
Groundwater	2,000,000 mi³ 8,336,000 km³	0.613	Deep wells for drinking and irrigation
Freshwater Lakes	30,000 mi³ 125,040 km³	0.009	Drinking water, irrigation water, recreation
Inland Seas	25,000 mi³ 104,200 km³	0.008	
Soil Moisture	16,000 mi³ 66,688 km³	0.005	Used by plants
Atmosphere	3,100 mi³ 12,921 km³	0.001	Clouds (ice crystals and rain)
Rivers	300 mi³ 1,250 km³	0.0001	Most of the water used by humans comes from rivers.
Total Water Volume	326,074,400 mi³ 1,359,078,099 km³	100 percent	

With the world population expected to top 8 billion people in the next thirty years, clean water shortages will result in new famines and disease. The competition for water could lead to regional wars.

The world's water picture seems dire, but it doesn't have to be. Water is recyclable. The hydrologic cycle continually recycles salty ocean water and turns it into freshwater and drops it on the land. The needed freshwater is there, and it keeps being replenished. What is needed are better ways to use and protect the freshwater we have.

Irrigation of crops accounts for about two-thirds of all the freshwater used in the world, but less than half of that irrigation water actually reaches the roots of crops. New technologies for crop irrigation could do much to stretch the world's water supplies. One technology is the drip irrigation system. Instead of flooding cropland with water, the drip system brings water directly to each plant. Such systems have been shown to cut water use by 30 to 70 percent while increasing crop yields by 20 to 90 percent. Wise use of water for irrigation is a win-win situation.

Conservation of domestic water is another area where big savings in water can be made. If everyone uses water at home wisely, per person water demand will be reduced as well as the demand for waste treatment. In the quest for adequate freshwater supplies in the future, everyone counts.

Drip irrigation is an effective method of conserving freshwater. Water flows through plastic tubes that lie on or under the ground. The water is directed straight to each plant, so little is wasted.

The hydrosphere is a small but remarkable part of the complex system of spheres we call planet Earth. Earth's hydrosphere is unique in the solar system. As far as we know, Earth is the only planet in the solar system to harbor life. The big difference between Earth and the other planets is abundant liquid water. Liquid water is the main substance of life. Our use of water makes us important links in the hydrologic cycle. Our use of water will determine our future.

GLOSSARY

centrifugal acceleration: the outward pulling effect, due to Earth's rotation, that creates a second tide on the opposite side of Earth from the Moon

crest: the high part of a wave

current: a riverlike flow moving through oceans

density: the mass of an object compared to the mass of an equal volume of freshwater

geyser: a periodic eruption of hot groundwater and steam onto Earth's surface

groundwater: water soaked into the soil and rock beneath Earth's surface

heat capacity: the ability of materials to store heat

high tide: the high point in ocean tides

hydrologic cycle: the pathway water takes as it changes from one form to another and travels around planet Earth

hydrosphere: the thin outer coating of water surrounding Earth

longshore current: a flow of water parallel to shorelines created by waves striking shorelines at an angle

low tide: the low point in ocean tides

permeability: the ability of solid materials to permit water to pass through them

porosity: the amount of holes in a solid material

salinity: the quantity of dissolved chemicals in seawater

stalactite: an icicle-like rock formation that grows from the ceiling of a cave

stalagmite: a cone-shaped rock formation that grows upward from the floor of a cave

tidal bore: waves created when tides move through constrictions in coastlines

transpiration: water given off to the atmosphere by plant leaves

trough: the low part of a wave

tsunami: powerful and destructive waves caused by earthquakes and massive landslides into the ocean

watershed: the extent of land that drains rain and snow meltwater into a river

water table: the upper surface of groundwater

wave: a rolling motion of the water surface usually created by wind

wave height: the distance between the crest and the trough of a wave

wavelength: the distance between two successive wave crests or wave troughs

SOURCE NOTE

68   "The Price of Optimism," *Time*, August 1, 1969.

BIBLIOGRAPHY

Bobick, J. E., ed. *The Handy Science Answer Book*. Centennial edition. Pittsburgh: Carnegie Library, 2005.

"The Earth from Space." *National Aeronautics and Space Administration*. n.d., http://earth.jsc.nasa.gov/sseop/efs/. (October 3, 2006).

"Earth's Water: Surface—water topics." *United States Geological Survey*. n.d., http://ga.water.usgs.gov/edu/mearthsw.html. (October 3, 2006).Hamblin, W. K. and Christiansen E. H. *Earth's Dynamic Systems*. Upper Saddle River, NJ: Prentice Hall, 2003.

Hutchinson, S., and L. Hawkins. *Oceans: A Visual Guide*. Sydney, Australia: Firefly Books, 2005.

Lambert, D., and the Diagram Group. *The Field Guide to Geology*. New York: Diagram Visual Information, 1988.

Luhr, J. F., ed. *Smithsonian Earth*. London: Dorling Kindersley, 2003.

Mathez, E. A., ed. *Earth Inside and Out, American Museum of Natural History Book*. New York: W. W. Norton & Company, 2001.

"Oceans." *World Watch Institute*. n.d., http://www.worldwatch.org/topics/nature/ocean (October 20, 2006).

Pinet, P. *Invitation to Oceanography*. 3rd ed., Boston: Jones and Bartlett Publishers, 2003.

Tarbuk, E. J., and F. K. Lutgens. *The Earth, Introduction to Physical Geology*. Columbus, OH: Merrill Publishing Company, 1990.

Tibballs, G. *Tsunami: The World's Most Terrifying Natural Disaster*. London: Carlton Book, 2005.

"Visible Earth." *National Aeronautics and Space Administration*. October 2005. http://visibleearth.nasa.gov (October 18, 2006).

FOR FURTHER INFORMATION

Books

Carruthers, M. *Glaciers*. New York: Scholastic, 2005.

Lindop, Laurie. *Venturing into the Deep Sea*. Minneapolis: Twenty-First Century Books, 2006.

MacQuitty, M. *Ocean*. New York: DK Publishing, 2003.

Nye, B. *Bill Nye: The Science Guy's Big Blue Ocean*. New York: Hyperion Books for Children, 2003.

Rapp, Val. *Life in a River: The Columbia River Basin*. Minneapolis: Twenty-First Century Books, 2003.

Steward, Melissa. *Life in a Lake: Lake Superior*. Minneapolis: Twenty-First Century Books, 2003.

Varukka, M., ed. *Scholastic Atlas of Oceans*. New York: Scholastic, 2004.

Woods, Michael, and Mary B. Woods. *Tsunamis*. Minneapolis: Lerner Publications Company, 2007.

Websites

National Snow and Ice Date Center. All about Glaciers.
http://nsidc.org/glaciers/index.html
A tour of the life of a glacier, quick facts, a photo gallery, and scientific data about glaciers.

UN-Oceans. U N Atlas of the Oceans.
http://www.oceansatlas.org/index.jsp
An information system provided by the United Nations for those wanting information about the world's oceans, their geography, their uses, and environmental and political issues relating to them.

U.S. Environmental Protection Agency. Wetlands, Oceans, and Watersheds information. http://www.epa.gov/owow/
A government site offering information about wetlands, oceans, and watersheds and how individual citizens can work to protect these resources.

U.S. Geological Survey. Water Science for Schools.
http://ga.water.usgs.gov/edu/
Information on many aspects of water, along with pictures, data, maps, and an interactive center.

Yellowstone National Park. The Geysers of Yellowstone.
http:www.yellowstone.net/geysers
Links to specific information about Yellowstone's various geyser
basins and Old Faithful, as well as the Yellowstone Caldera.
Check out the video gallery to see the geysers in action.

INDEX

ABOUT THE AUTHOR

Gregory L. Vogt holds a doctor of education degree in curriculum and instruction from Oklahoma State University. He began his professional career as a science teacher. He later joined NASA's education programs teaching students and teachers about space exploration. He works in outreach programs for the Kennedy Space Center. He also serves as an educational consultant to Delaware North Parks Services of Spaceport and is the principal investigator for an educational grant with the National Space Biomedical Research Institute. Vogt has written more than seventy children's science books.

PHOTO ACKNOWLEDGMENTS